11/12/14

Louisburg Library District No. 1

206 S. Broadway

Louisburg, KS. 66053

913-837-2217

www.louisburglibrary.org

When I Grow Up

I CAN BE AN ASTRONAUT

By Alex Appleby

Gareth Stevens
PUBLISHING

Please visit our website, www.garethstevens.com. For a free color catalog of all our high-quality books, call toll free 1-800-542-2595 or fax 1-877-542-2596.

Library of Congress Cataloging-in-Publication Data

Appleby, Alex.
I can be an astronaut / by Alex Appleby.
p. cm. — (When I grow up)
Includes index.
ISBN 978-1-4824-0755-6 (pbk.)
ISBN 978-1-4824-1007-5 (6-pack)
ISBN 978-1-4824-0754-9 (library binding)
1. Astronauts — Juvenile literature. 2. Astronautics — Vocational guidance — Juvenile literature. I. Appleby, Alex.
II. Title.
TL793.A66 2015
629.45—d23

First Edition

Published in 2015 by
Gareth Stevens Publishing
111 East 14th Street, Suite 349
New York, NY 10003

Copyright © 2015 Gareth Stevens Publishing

Editor: Ryan Nagelhout
Designer: Sarah Liddell

Photo credits: Cover, p. 1 (astronaut) glenda/Shutterstock.com; cover, p. 1 (stars) Procy/Shutterstock.com; p. 5 njaj/Shutterstock.com; p. 7 bikeriderlondon/Shutterstock.com; p. 9 iurii/Shutterstock.com; p. 11 Jacobs Stock Photography/Photographer's Choice/Getty Images; p. 13 vicspacewalker/Shutterstock.com; pp. 15, 24 (rocket) Fer Gregory/Shutterstock.com; p. 17 NASA/Handout/Getty Images News/Getty Images; p. 19 Michael Dunning/ Photographer's Choice/Getty Images; pp. 21, 24 (Earth) mrgao/iStock/Thinkstock.com; p. 23 Space Frontiers/ Stringer/Archive Photos/Getty Images; p. 24 (moon) hkeita/iStock/Thinkstock.com.

Printed in the United States of America

CPSIA compliance information: Batch #CS15GS: For further information contact Gareth Stevens, New York, New York at 1-800-542-2595.

Contents

I love space!

I want to go there!

Many people
have been in space.
They are
called astronauts.

I want to be one
when I grow up.

11

They train very hard.

They go to space
in a rocket.

15

They study things
in space.

Some went
to the moon!

19

They saw Earth
from far away.

21

I want to go
to other planets!

23

Words to Know

Earth

moon

rocket

Index